DISCARDED

SCIENCE AT WORK

ELEMENTS

AT DISCARDED

WORK

LAUREN KUKLA

Consulting Editor, Diane Craig, M.A./Reading Specialist

Sandcastle

An Imprint of Abdo Publishing
abdopublishing.com

abdopublishing.com

Published by Abdo Publishing, a division of ABDO, PO Box 398166, Minneapolis, Minnesota 55439. Copyright © 2017 by Abdo Consulting Group, Inc. International copyrights reserved in all countries. No part of this book may be reproduced in any form without written permission from the publisher. SandCastle™ is a trademark and logo of Abdo Publishing.

Printed in the United States of America, North Mankato, Minnesota
062016
092016

THIS BOOK CONTAINS
RECYCLED MATERIALS

Design: Mighty Media, Inc.
Content Developer: Nancy Tuminelly
Production: Mighty Media, Inc.
Editor: Liz Salzmann
Photo Credits: Shutterstock

Library of Congress Cataloging-in-Publication Data

Names: Kukla, Lauren, author. | Craig, Diane.
Title: Elements at work / Lauren Kukla ; consulting editor, Diane Craig,
    M.A., reading specialist.
Description: Minneapolis, Minnesota : Abdo Publishing, [2017] | Series:
    Science at work
Identifiers: LCCN 2016000310 (print) | LCCN 2016002724 (ebook) | ISBN
    9781680781403 (print) | ISBN 9781680775839 (ebook)
Subjects: LCSH: Chemical elements--Juvenile literature.
Classification: LCC QD466 .K85 2017 (print) | LCC QD466 (ebook) | DDC
    546--dc23
LC record available at http://lccn.loc.gov/2016000310

SandCastle™ Level: Fluent

SandCastle™ books are created by a team of professional educators, reading specialists, and content developers around five essential components—phonemic awareness, phonics, vocabulary, text comprehension, and fluency—to assist young readers as they develop reading skills and strategies and increase their general knowledge. All books are written, reviewed, and leveled for guided reading, early reading intervention, and Accelerated Reader™ programs for use in shared, guided, and independent reading and writing activities to support a balanced approach to literacy instruction. The SandCastle™ series has four levels that correspond to early literacy development. The levels are provided to help teachers and parents select appropriate books for young readers.

EMERGING · BEGINNING · TRANSITIONAL · FLUENT

CONTENTS

ABOUT ELEMENTS

Have you ever watched a balloon float? Or cooked on a **charcoal** grill?

You saw
elements
at work!

What are elements?

They are the simplest forms of something. Gold is one. So is iron.

Many scientists have studied elements.
Dmitri Mendeleyev sorted them.
He made a table.

Marie Curie was another scientist.
She found two new elements.

Zinc is an element. So is **copper**.
Both are in pennies.

Chase holds balloons. The **helium** inside makes them float.

Atoms make up elements. Atoms
are tiny. They are in everything.

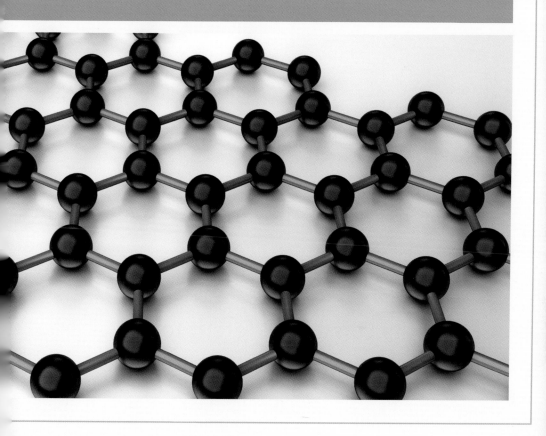

An element has
one kind of atom.

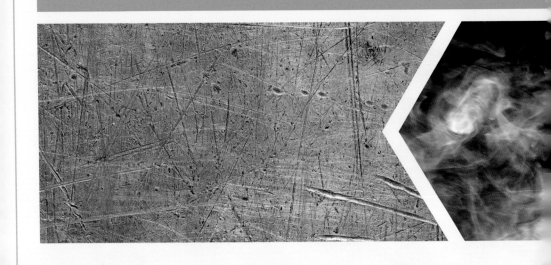

Elements come in different forms.
They can be metals. Some are liquids.

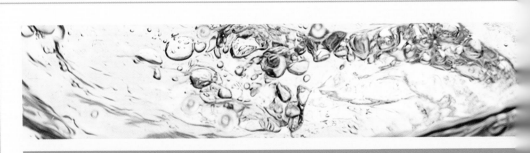

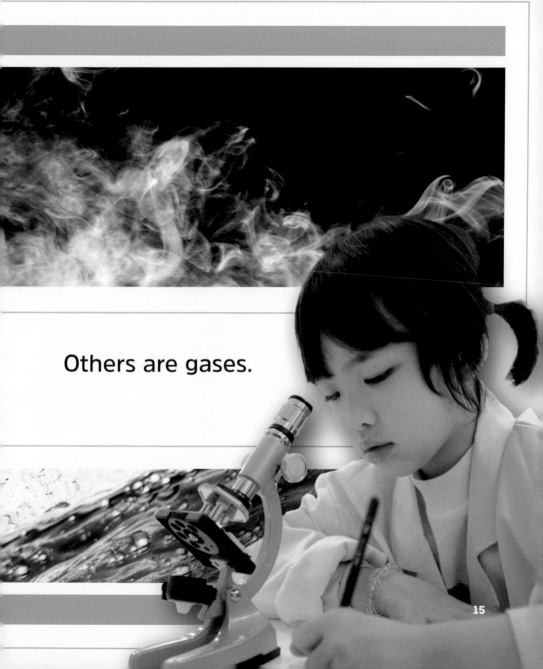

Others are gases.

Sometimes elements change
form. **Carbon** can be coal.

It can also be a **diamond**!
The atoms are the same.

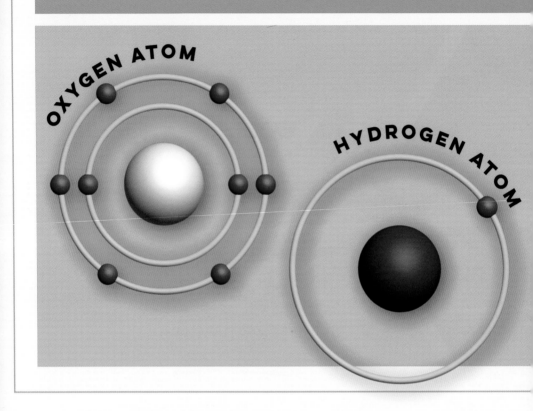

Atoms of two or more
elements can combine.

Oxygen and **hydrogen** are elements. Together they make water.

Today we know of 118 elements.

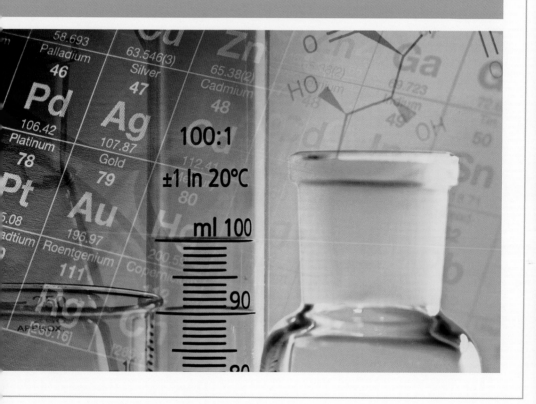

But there may be more!

THINK ABOUT IT

Look around you! Where else are
elements at work? How do you use them?

GLOSSARY

carbon – an element found in all plants and animals.

charcoal – incompletely burned wood.

copper – a reddish-brown element that is usually metal.

diamond – a shiny, clear stone used to make jewelry.

helium – an element that is a light, colorless gas.

hydrogen – an element that is a colorless, odorless gas.

oxygen – a colorless gas found in air and water.

zinc – an element that is usually a blue and white metal.